WITCHCRAFT

COLORING BOOK

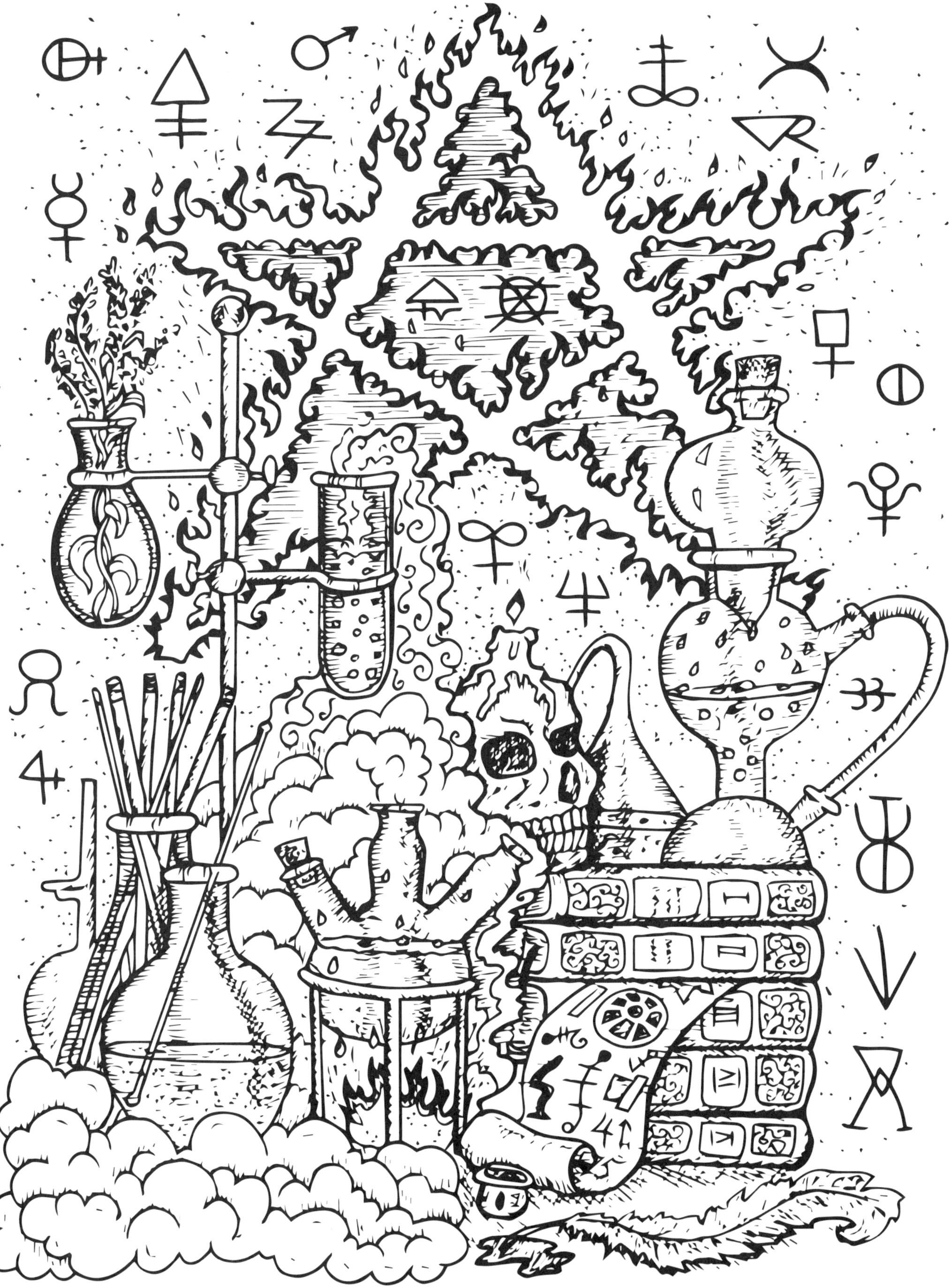

R.I.P
12 1 2 3 4
Carpe Diem

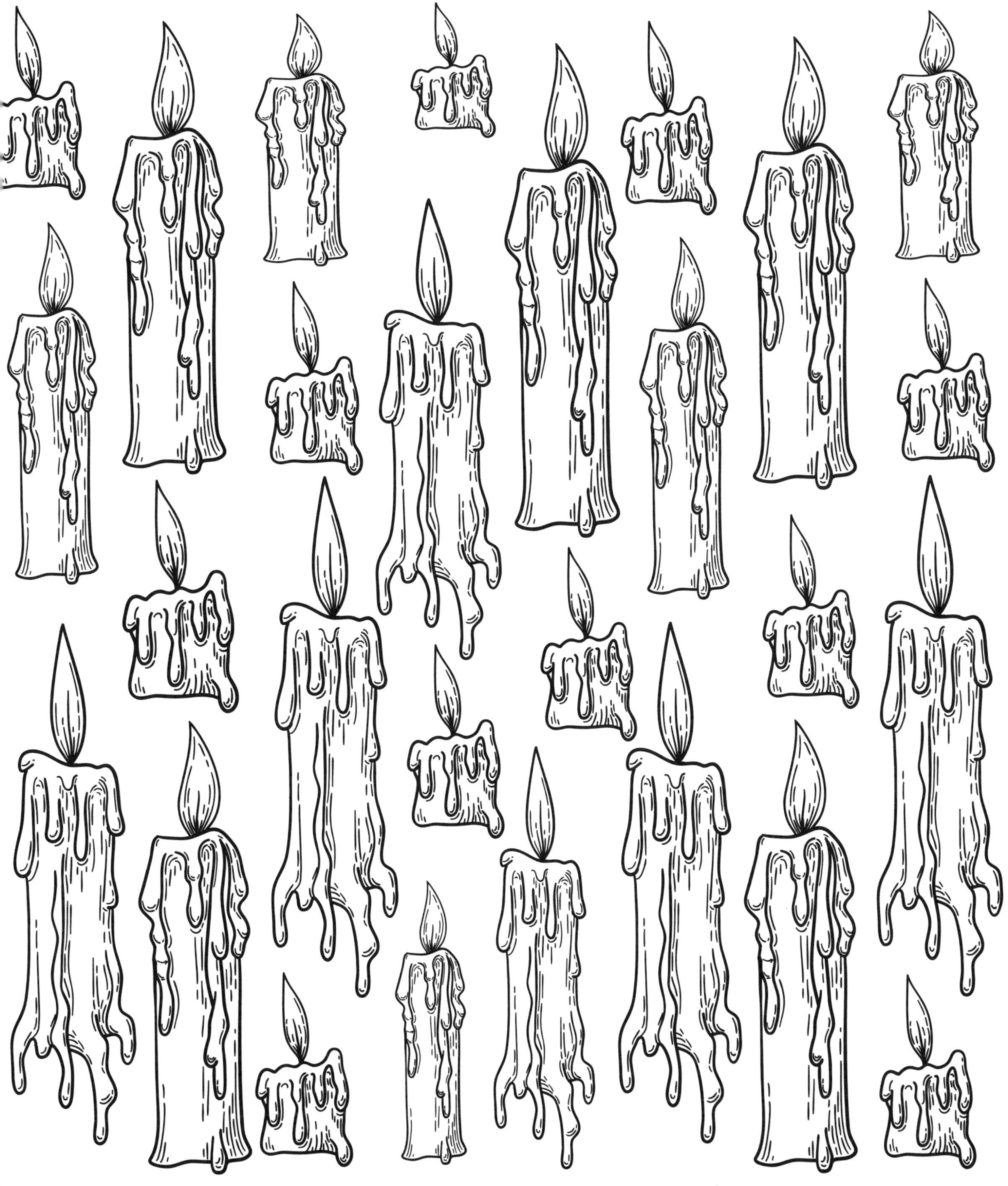

02
01
03
00

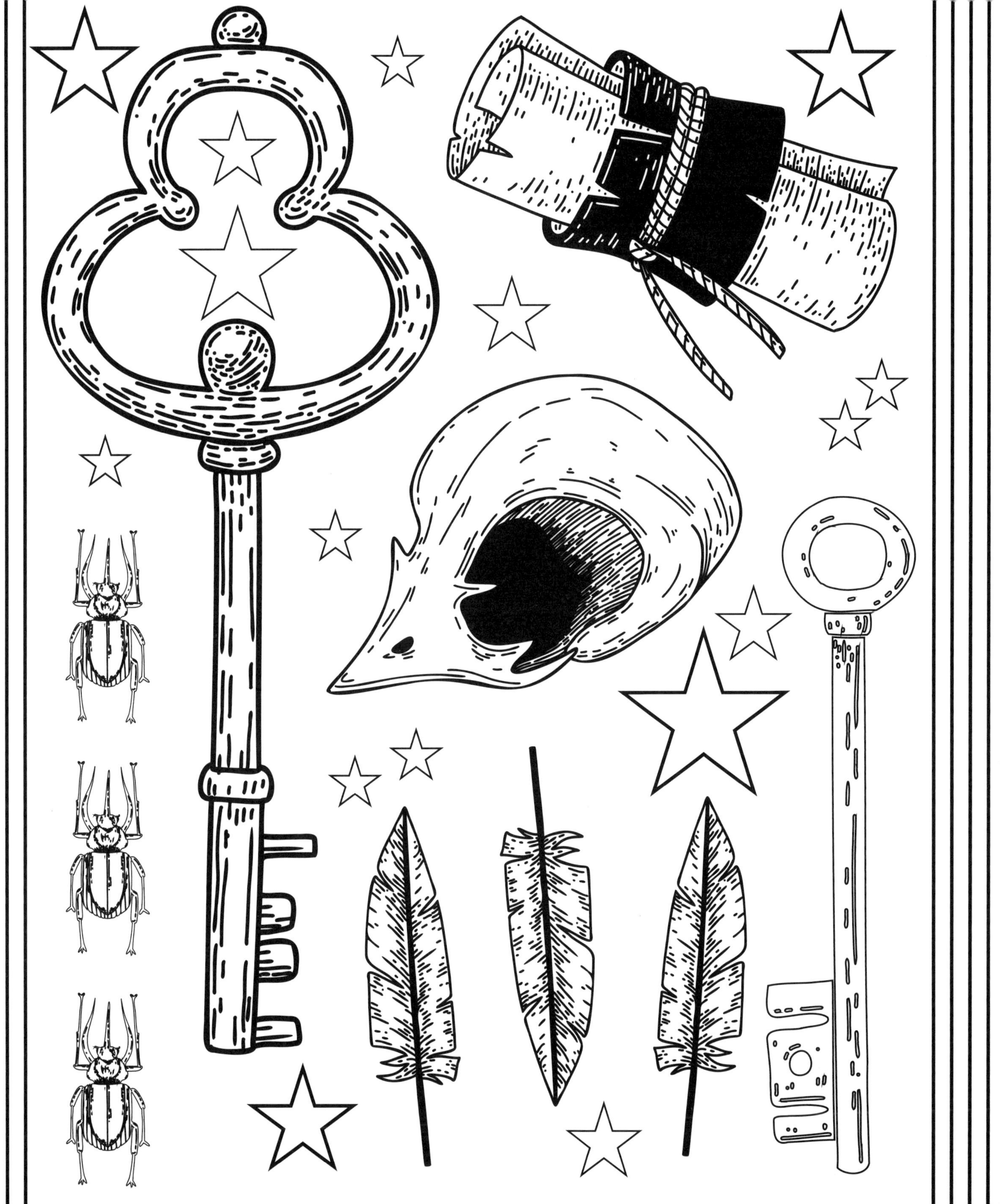

Nascentes Morimur

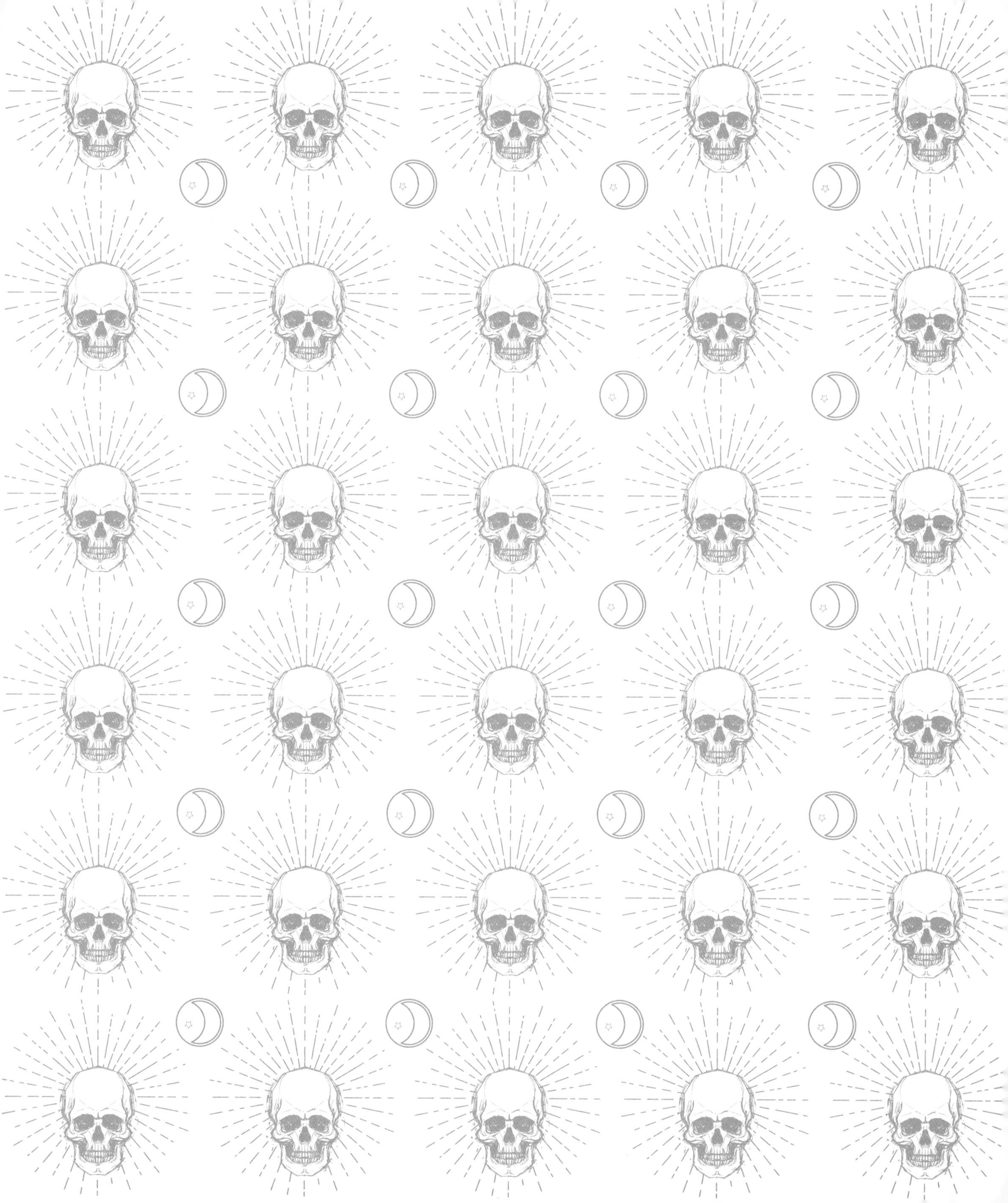

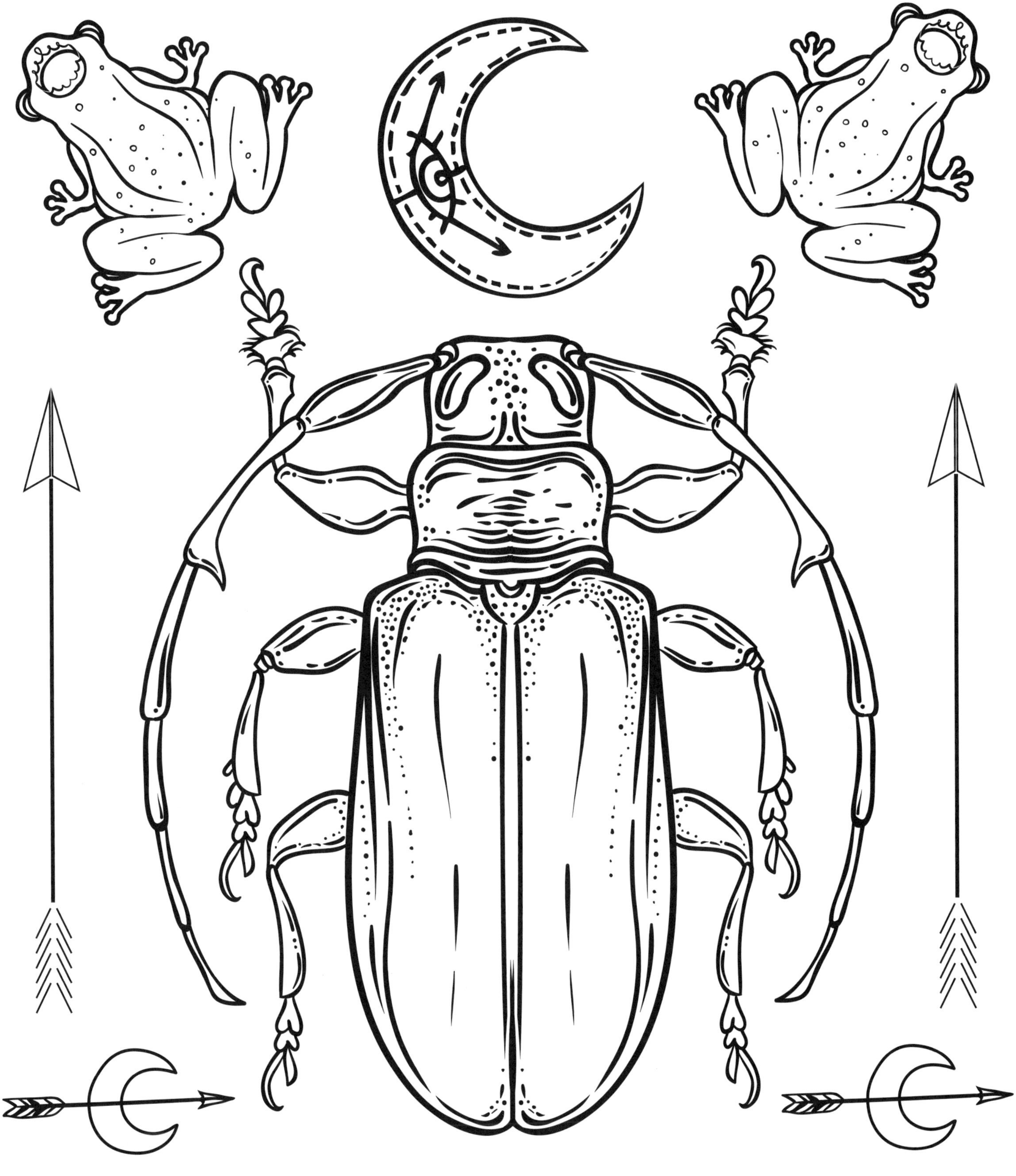

CATS
M
SPELLS
WITCH
RECIPES
POTIONS
XXXIII.

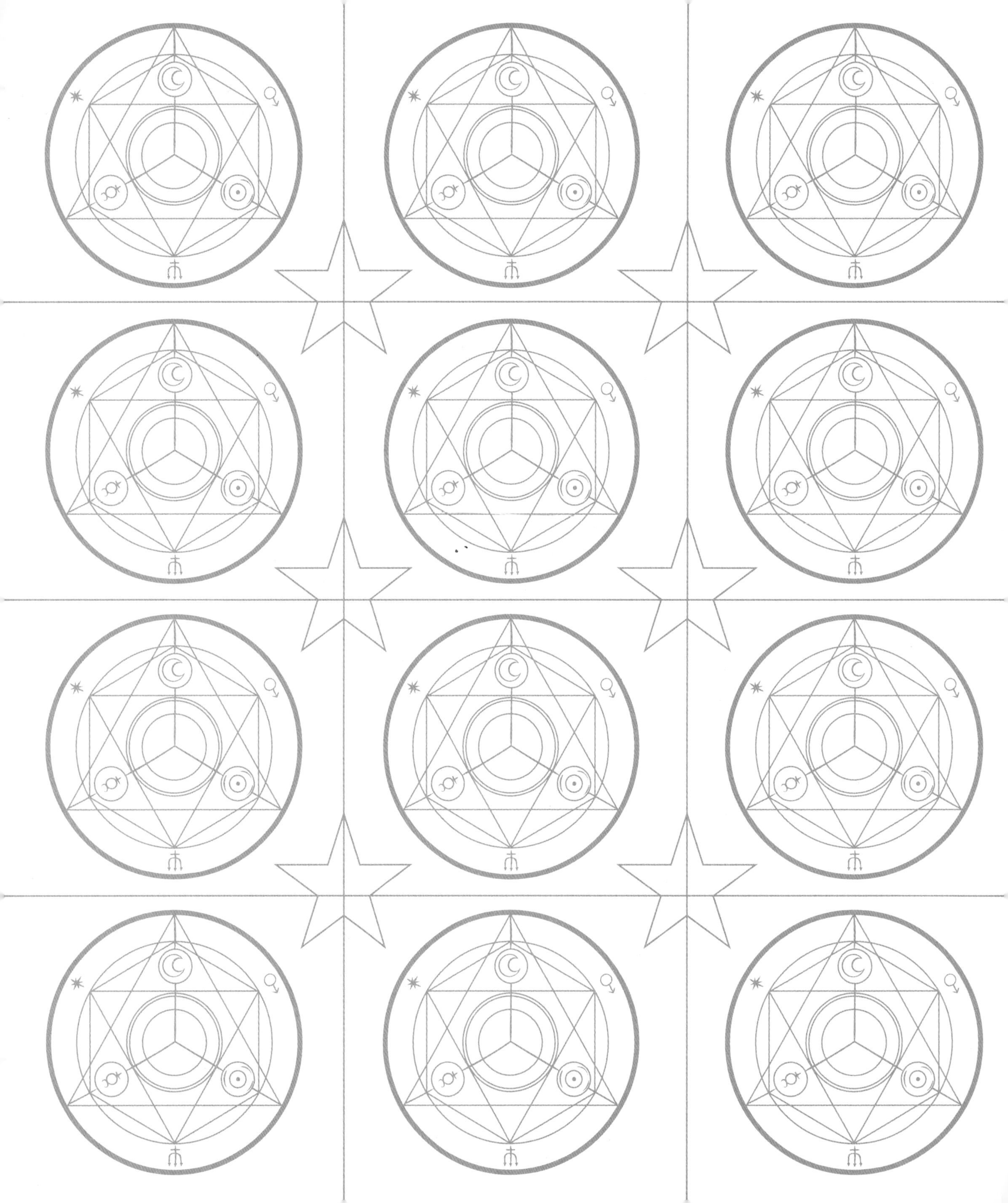

EMBRACING YOUR INNER
WITCH

The Magician

Death

रं

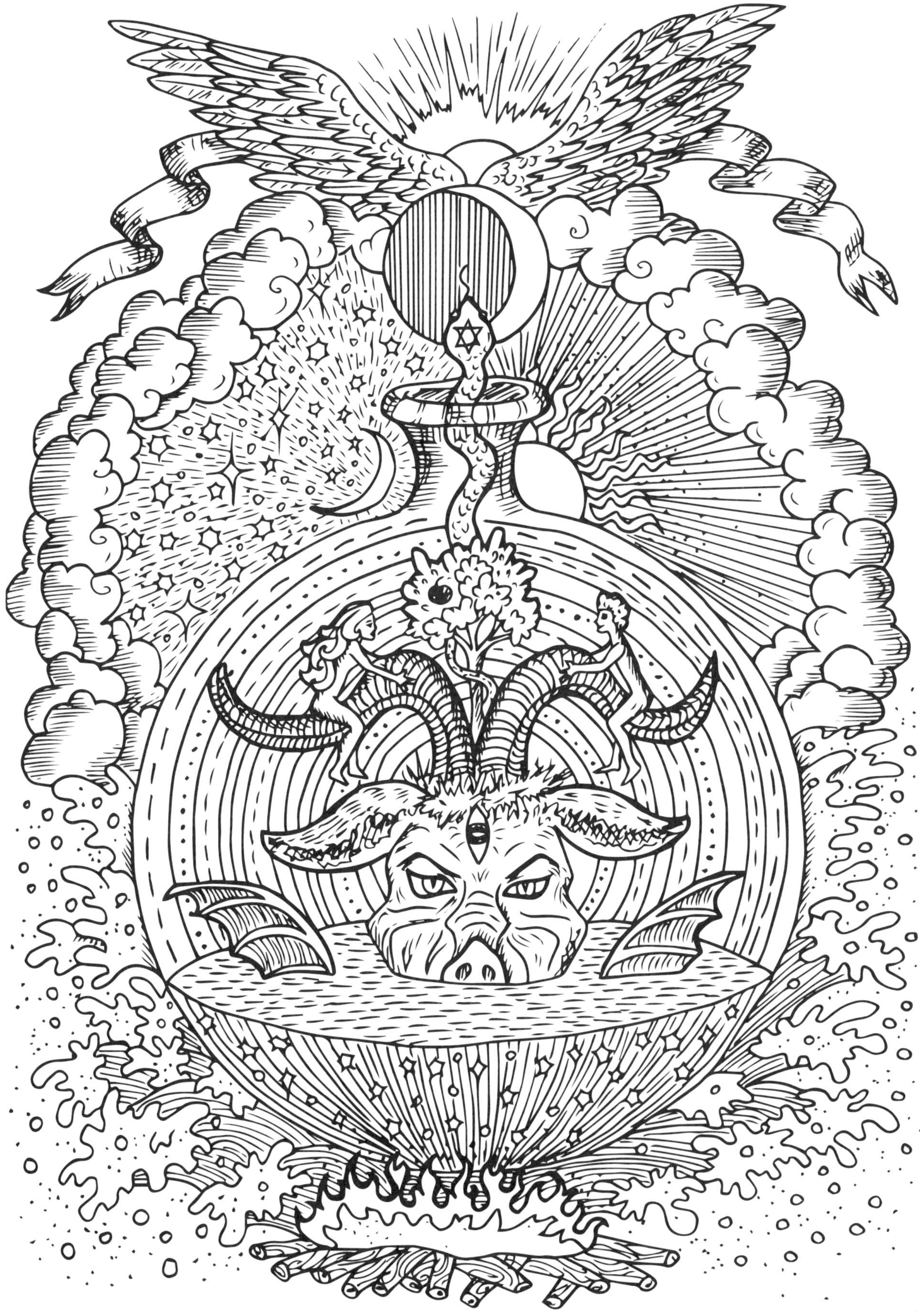

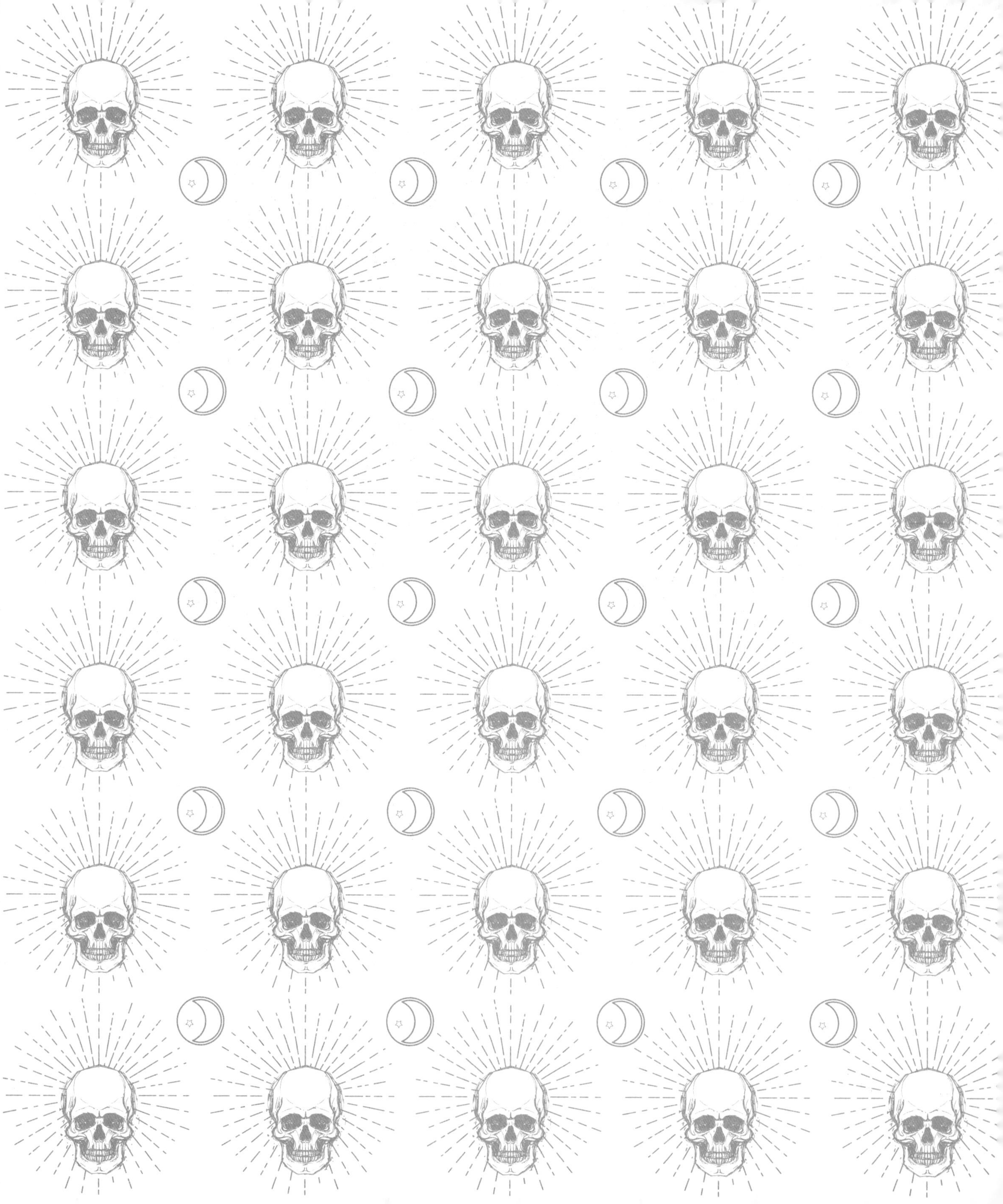

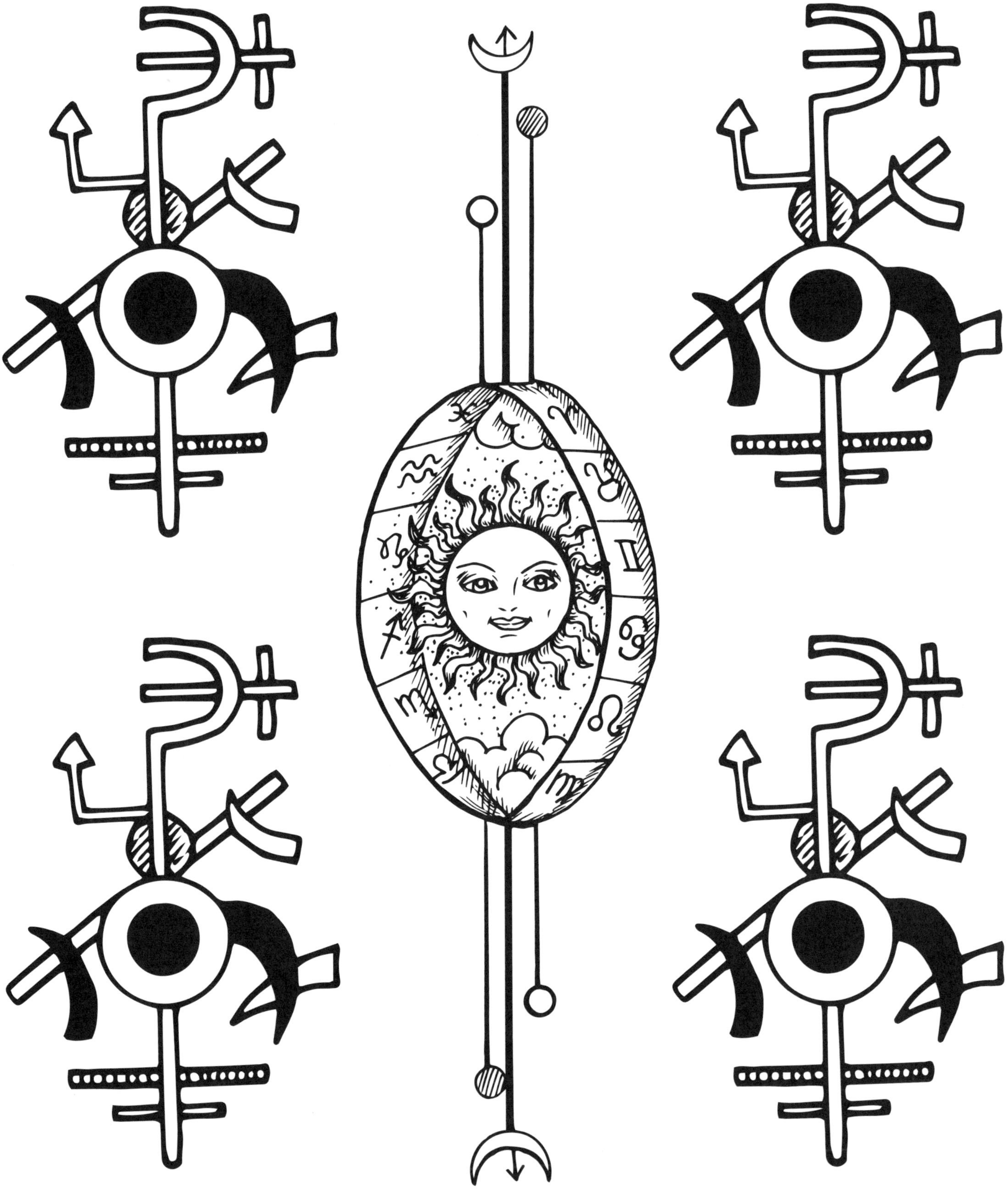

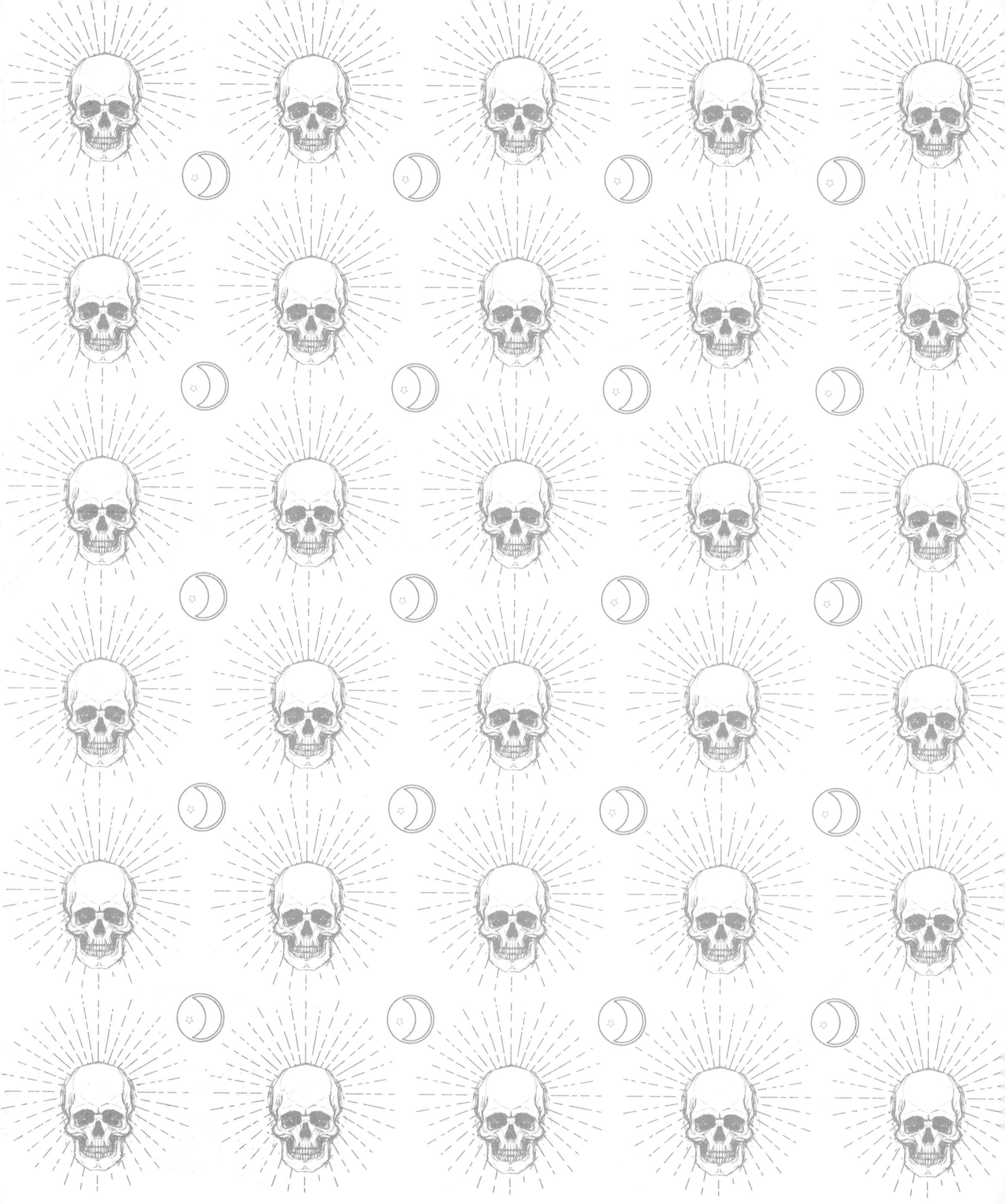

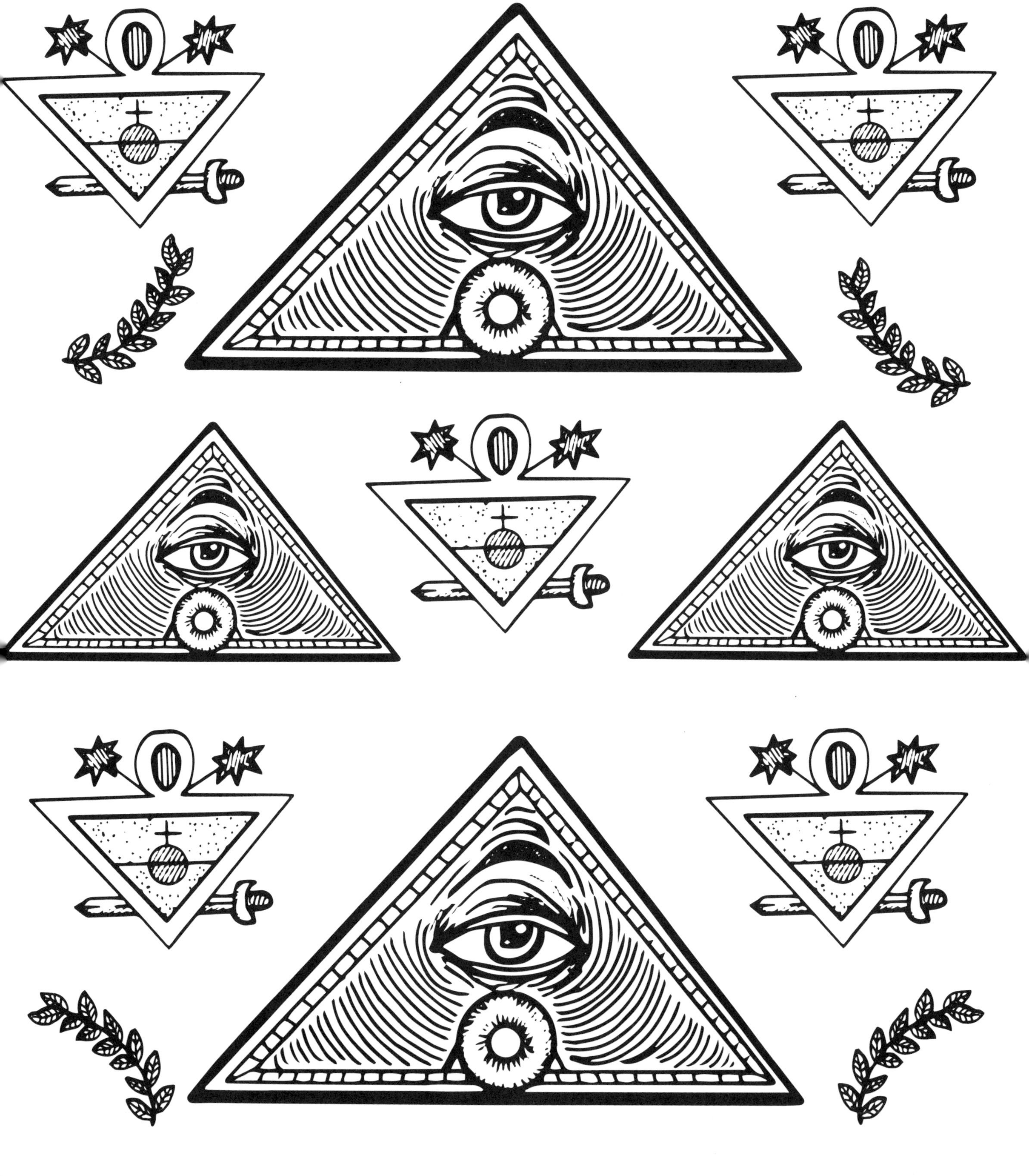

XVIII
The Moon

The Sun

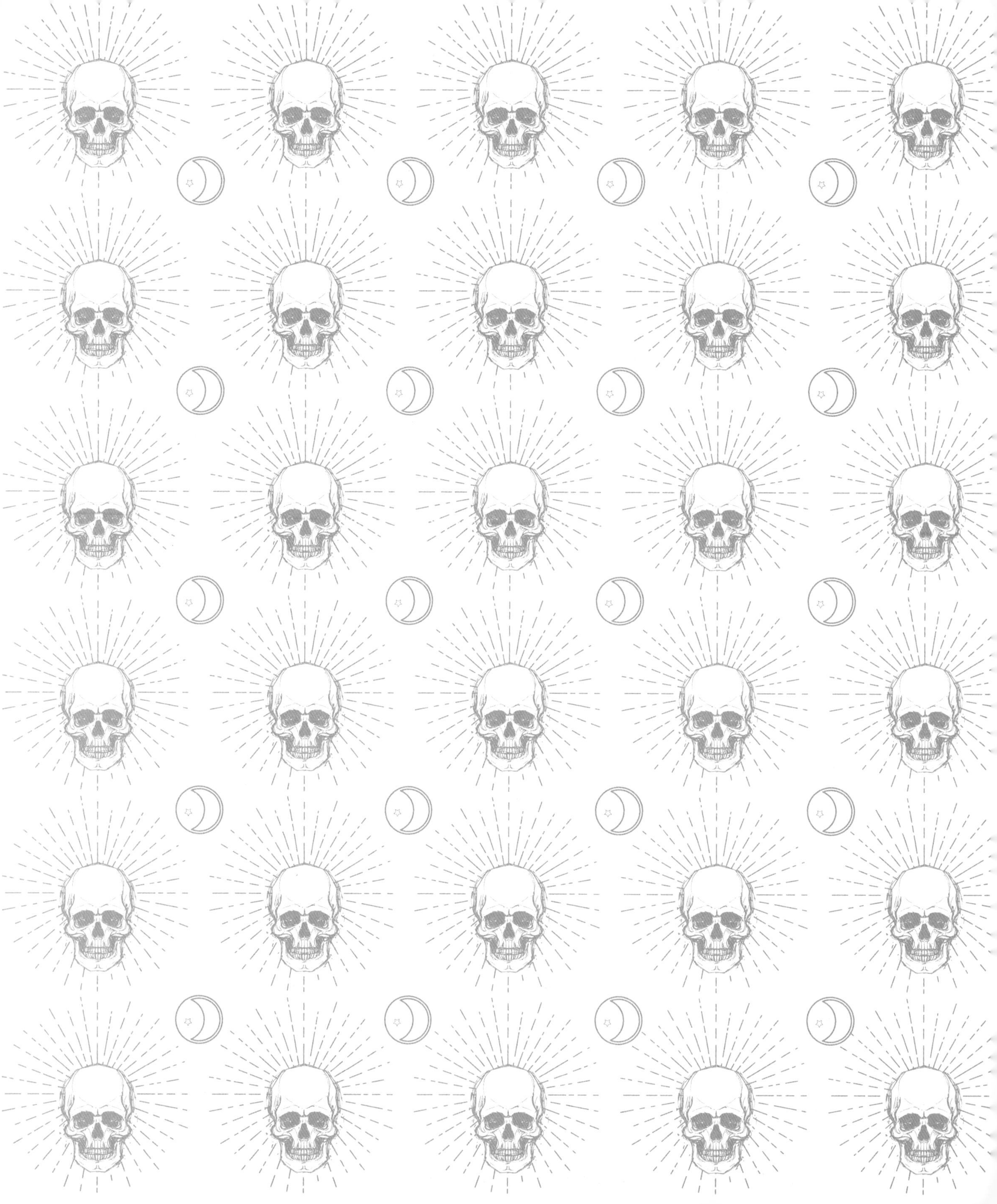

DREAM POTION

DRINK up

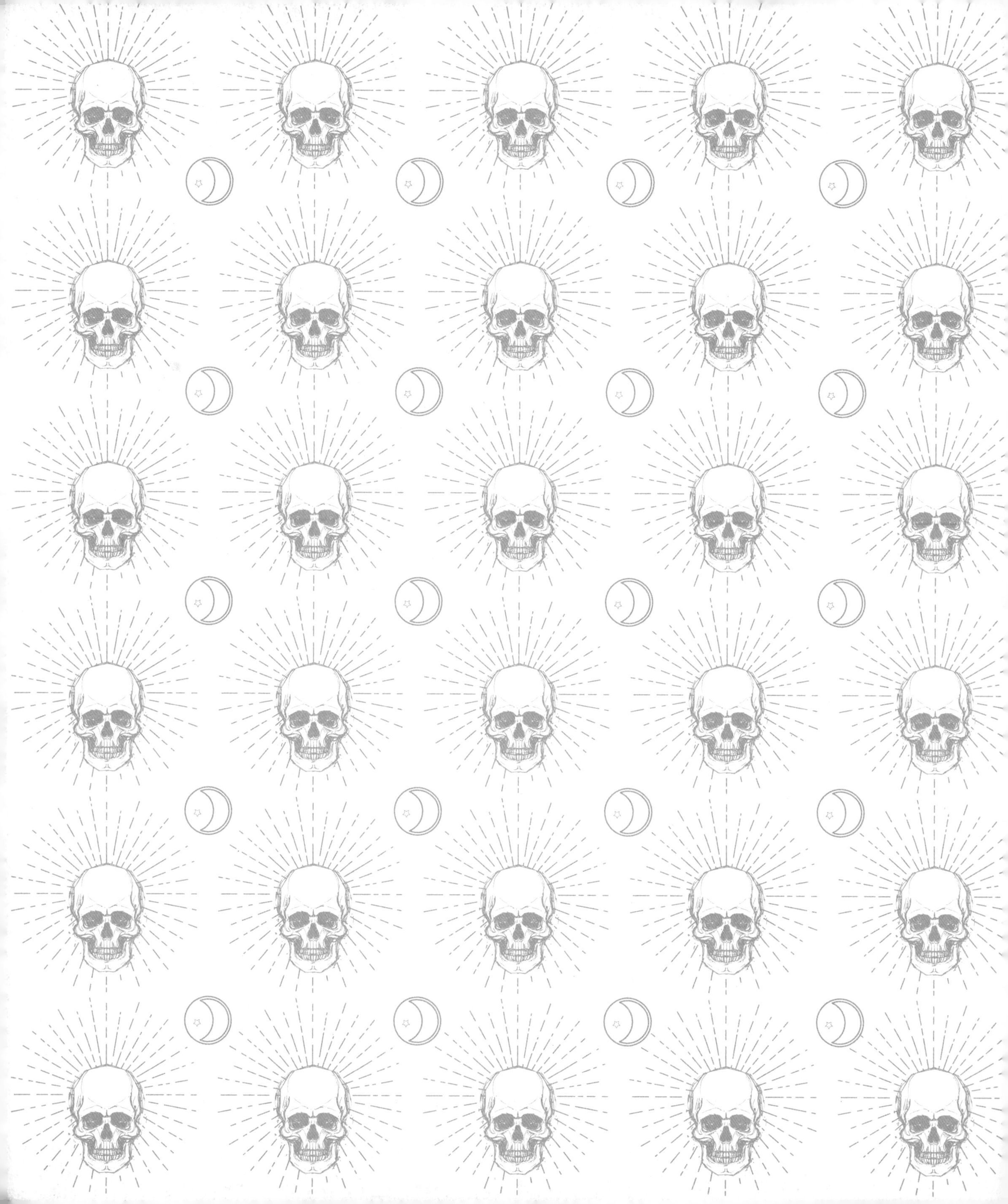